inner peace: *an abc*

inner peace: *an abc*

Raj Arumugam

..inner peace is never lost; it's always there just below the apparent surface of discord. One simply dives deep enough to see this peace that pervades and that never leaves one, though one may be distracted by insistent diversions...

inner peace: an abc

Inner peace is effortless, as it's always there within.
One just has to see it.

And once one truly sees this inner peace – not with words or just intellectually, but when one actually sees this inner peace within – it is one's, always; no one takes away that…

Nothing and no evil and no violent force or even the most difficult of circumstances in one's life can remove that inner peace that one sees within; but let one see this not as a word, or as a phrase but as an actuality.

Feel that peace, see that inner peace and let it radiate always –
for it is the harmony within each and it is always one's own.

A

Let amity be your constant companion….Be at peace with all beings, equally at peace with those near and those far, and thus walk hand in hand with amity as in a bounteous garden…

B

 Be mindful of your blessings always…To be alive, to breathe
in fresh air; and to be with the family and in the
companionship of good fellow-human beings; and the kindness
of strangers; and the creatures of this world and the flowers
that bloom, and to have a place in this marvelous planet of
ours….all these too are blessings….

There is a life of the body in the domain of the physical, and the legitimate needs of the body are just as important as one's inner needs…

C

Think critically....even while we love and are at peace with the world, do not forget to think critically for oneself so that one is not the fool of the cunning...and thus thinking for oneself carefully and critically one keeps one's time and energy and one's own mind....

Do your own thinking; allowing others to do your thinking for you is to systematically lose one's will to live life to its fullest...

Freshness comes when one discards clichés in word, thought and deed – and with freshness comes vigor, steadiness and wisdom….

Though one may mature and grow in intellect, let the child be in you always. For each moment in which one ceases to be a child, one is but walking dead.

D

Death is only part of a process in our lives….it is but another phase as is one's birth….

Witness the wonder of this process and constant change, and marvel at it as one marvels at sunset and sunrise – and thus is there no agony or ecstasy but quiet and cool contemplation of birth, our day to day living and death….the whole of which is life...

Die to each moment; die to each memory and die to each event and each day - and thus is there constant renewal and the ever new, and so one sees for oneself there is truly no fear in death.

Each of one of us has many levels or dimensions of being human that are open to us:

- Life in touch with the universal
- Life of the mind
- The aesthetic life
- The creative life
- The emotional/affective domain
- The physical life/life of the senses

The full life is one in which we seek to *enjoy, develop* and to be *fully actualized* in all aspects of our being. Some people, for various reasons, may try and suppress and deny themselves a life in one area and focus on another. This sort of suppression and restraint will cause harm to oneself over the long run. It can also lead to hypocrisy and deception. On the other hand, some people pay undue attention to one area neglecting other areas, and again cause themselves a great deal of mental and possibly physical harm.

Enjoy life in all domains – but *aim for balance.*

E

…equanimity is priceless…there is no need for wildness in joy or agony; as the tides come and go so do our mental states, and all that we consider bad or good….like the rise of the moon, or the coming of the stars and the going of the stars are our emotions and our lives and our happiness and sorrows….see them for what they are and equanimity dwells shining within one always….

F

The free mind is the greatest blessing….Be free of conditioning and be free of propaganda; be free of identity and of the group, and one is truly free; be free of the past in all its forms as it arises in the mind as remembrance of hurts and wrongs, and be free of the future as it arises as constant planning and anticipation and unnecessary tension….

But what is the free mind? One is not free who allows it to be defined for one.

Be free of anyone who will teach you: there is no relative freedom – only complete freedom…

During one's meeting or interaction with another being – any being, human or creature - be mindful of the question: *Am I fair to this being?*

And after one's meeting or interaction with another being – any being, human or creature - be mindful of the question: *Have I been fair to this being?*

G

There is grace in your heart, in your mind and in your very
being…delve deep within and see it - let it glow, and that grace
will show in the smoothness of your very movement and
speech; and that grace will flow in your manner, and that grace
will fill your life and each moment with peace, charm and
joy….

God? I have no use for God as I have no use for clichés.

The only reality is Love. God is just another word.

H

Neglect no aspect of your being – for each aspect of your being is necessary and good.

Find for yourself all dimensions of your being…see what happens and what you need in each dimension…be moderate and sufficient in each dimension, and so there will be no tension in any of the dimensions of your being, and thus harmony is yours….

I

Insight is when you can see beyond words and the intellect…as when one feels the presence of love and wisdom...let your insight and your intuition live and flourish – for to suppress it is to deny yourself wisdom and inner light…

Words are useless and mislead in the inner life and therefore it is in the light of insight and intuition that one has direct seeing of what actually is….

J

Rejoice in the joys of others...rejoice in the happiness of others…rejoice in your own joy…find the joy within yourself and the joy in the world…

Be fair and just – not so that one may be loved by others or so one may escape punishment or so one may enter heaven, but be just for its own intrinsic beauty.

K

There is a kingdom within that is not by any other but of oneself….there is chaos there if one rules unwisely, and there is joy and harmony if one enters in wisdom….peace and harmony radiate there in that kingdom of your own wisdom, and not by the power or grace or authority or wisdom of others…No being, however mighty and however supernatural, can effect order in there…The kingdom is only of oneself and yet in oneness…

Enter therefore your own kingdom wisely, enter in your own wisdom…

L

All that there is in the world is love….All the many and countless words and revelations and traditions and systems are all but love….

All the world's Holy Books and Revelations and Sermons are useless – there is only love…

The love in which there is conflict or tension, the love in which one seeks to own or possess or to carve out a territory or group or personal identity or salvation or gain or protection – that is not love…

The love that includes all and that excludes none, the love that knows no hate or violence or tension or expectation or punishment or reward – that is love….

We have allowed the idea and myth of God to replace the reality of Love: forget this illusion about God, for the only reality is Love…

We are liars…we are drugged by lies and
addicted to lies…but while it is easy to see the lies told to one
or the lies one tells others, it is more difficult to see the lies one
tells oneself…

M

Be mindful of the moment….be mindful of one's breath – of the breath as one exhales, as one inhales…be mindful of the emotion or thought that arises, that lives and that subsides…

….with no censure, no judgment, no labels, no memory-making and cherishing of experiences…be mindful too of walking or of sitting; be mindful of each act and thought…

And so does one live the moment and so thought and time - the past and future - lose their tyrannical hold on the mind…

…there are a flower, the sky and the setting sun; rock and two fish, air, land and water; there is mind that perceives, stays like a still lake, as reflective as an un-possessive mirror…

N

Be mindful too of the nuances of the words we utter and use; be mindful of the nuances of one's speech and actions and one's silence and one's inaction…

O

Observe with no imprint...observe with no judgment or residue...observe what actually is...

observing a tree

You see the tree....see what is; see it as it is, not with all of one's conditioning...you look...one does not form a judgment and an attachment and a craving for a repetition of this event - but just observe, with no labels...no naming...one sees what is there before one without a name, for the name is the past...just observe what is...

observing the mind

One observes what is – one observes one's mind, oneself - not as what authority says one is, but as one actually sees oneself; direct and straight seeing oneself...

One sees oneself without the conditioning and with no prejudice; one sees what actually is...

One observes the activities of the mind…one sees the emotion or thought that arises, as it lives and as it subsides…one does not name the emotion or thought, for to do so is to bring in conditioning which is the tyranny of thought; one does not label it and one does not feel guilt or like or dislike…one merely observes what actually is…

One who observes one's mind knows oneself – not oneself as some abstract and superhuman eternal entity, but as one *is*….Not second-hand - but directly, for oneself...

Not as what tradition or scriptures or science or reports tell us what we are – but as one actually observes and as one sees what *is*…

How can one know anything without knowing oneself? Of what use is your knowing of all that you know without self-knowledge as you actually are, and not according to some theory or report or ideology?

P

There are things and events you have control of – and how you pace these that are within your control determines how much peace and quiet there is in your heart…

Know then the rhythm at which your mind moves and pace the events you have control of at this rhythm…

For things one has no control of, one's wisdom will bring a harmony between one and what faces one…

..inner peace is never lost; it's always there just below the apparent surface of discord. One simply dives deep enough to see this peace that pervades and that never leaves one, though one may be distracted by insistent diversions...

…a walk brings peace; a walk brings quiet and bliss…a walk brings energy and silence and hope, brightness and balance….

…walk in silence amongst the trees and the woods…there are no objectives in this walk…let it be a walk of love…of that love between oneself and life…of that love in oneself, in nature – of love in the world…

…if you walk alone, it is good to walk without all that chatter in one's mind; if you walk with a friend or partner,
it is good to walk in silence…… let there be silence as one walks – silence within one, and between oneself and one's companions…rather, see for yourself how one is but part of the world as you walk…be part of the nature that surrounds you as you walk…
…observe the trees and the plants and the very path one walks on…observe the very flowers that greet one in one's walk….there is no need to remark on the beauty or quiet or the special-ness of the place one walks in…one just walks, being part of the world one is in…

 …just observe, and meet the trees and the woods and the flowers and the fields that greet one in one's walk…

…a walk brings peace; a walk brings quiet and bliss…a walk brings energy and silence and hope, brightness and balance….

Q

It may seem one's life is a quest and one searches and searches - and yet in that moment of awareness, of full attention, one sees there is no search, there is no arriving – for it is always there, it is always here and now…

There is no such thing as a quest; there is no such thing as a search…

R

 Rest well….one forgets in one's hurry that simple rest can revitalize and bring freshness…

S

Speak gently, speak with love; speak words that soothe and heal, and with no intent to hurt.
Speak words that bring amity, calm and peace and not words that promote division, anarchy and discord.

…one comes to the trees, to nature…one comes to the water, to the ocean, and one observes…without a companion, without chatter and with bodily stillness, and with no projection of one's own expectations and conditioning, one observes…one sees what is before one…and in that moment, in that instant, there is no one there with an identity; no one coming from the past to say: *this is what I am; this is what I did – and this was done to me; and such a person did this*; and in that moment, in that observing, in that seeing of the trees, of the ocean, of the water, in the seeing of what is before one, there is none that asserts its identity; there is none to speak of its name and its nationality and its pride and associations and its past, and there is none to reach out for a future: there is the moment, the stillness, the silence…

T

Thought may be the remembrance of cultures and technology that move societies forward, but thought can be mostly of the past that is a burden...

Be free of the past then and make no memory of it; for the past restricts and narrows and confines, and not making a memory of it is freedom....

…they are there; this is what is before one…one observes what is…one sees the shape and the spread or what is presented: the contours the light and the order and the chaos; one does not claim this; there is no commentary, no comparison, but being with what is before one…there is no theory or tradition, there is no naming of the species or history; there is no categorization, there is no effort or motive and no memory is made: *one sees what is; it is there…*

...see this thought; actually see it; observe this thought and its power and hold on one; there is the stretch of the mind and a thought arises there and it lives and links and brings in another, thought patterns, mental formations: a thought arises, it lives and fades and disappears...see this thought; observe the thought - without a label, without judgment or category or a name and any idea that *this is good*, or *this is bad*...

...just observe and see the thought; the duration of its life, even as it arises, as it lives and fades: just observe...see it...what happens?
...no, do not seek an answer in another: see your own thought; observe it yourself and see what actually is...see that thought; observe...do not hold on, but just observe and cling not to what you have learned; without knowing yourself there is no knowing anything...observe that thought, that idea...

U

The world's systems and hierarchy and Revelations aspire to drag everyone into uniformity and mediocrity...

To lead or to follow is to be mediocre – and the mediocre cannot allow independence...

This world of set formulas and systems despises free inquiry and wants to see each one of us the same in mind and habit and thought: it demands we crawl into its traditions and prescribed or revealed creed, and to fit into what it teaches is the way to be...

The world says this is the way things are and expects one to conform or to break...

Know what you are, know yourself - or the world subtly but swiftly transforms you into itself...

See what actually is rather than going the set ways of what one likes it to be or what should or ought to be or what is described to be ...Discard all authority and see for yourself what actually is...

V

Let there be vigor in all things one does; let there be vigor in thought, in one's inquiry, in one's speech and in one's works and deeds.

The most inspired moment in one's life is when vision unfolds naturally within; dullness comes of conditioning and beliefs that are the companions of complacent inquiry.

W

There is no treasure like the treasure of wisdom for with wisdom one sees the unmediated truth of life and the radiant truth of lasting joy in all circumstances.

Wide is the world and yet we seek to cut it and to confine it
and to create borders; wide is the mind and yet many seek
to constrict it and to set up boundaries and to restrict its space.

…a quiet walk did no one harm; away from the clamor and the ambitions and leaving the clutter and vanities, a walk in the silence and amongst the trees and just being with the colors and the feel and the texture of the trunks; and being with the tender touch of the branches that reach out to one when solitude is crisp silence; all these being simply part of oneself and one's calm and peace; walk then, now, in this and in these ample grounds below the trees and observing the gentle leaves; let us enter the wholeness that is ours…

When I see these woods and these flowers, says the companion, *I feel so at peace.*

Is this peace, dear friend, says the other, *is it come of the woods and flowers? Or is it possible that there is peace within oneself, with or without the woods?*

X

Avoid extremes in all matters – for it is the wisdom of moderation that universally promotes balance, health, happiness and calm.

Y

In one's intellect let there be maturity and completeness and
the wisdom of ages; but in one's inquiry into life let there be
vigor and newness and perennial youth.

Z

There are no confined zones in true love: love knows no boundaries and love knows no borders – the wide universe is the very home of love.

That inner peace radiates in the stars and in the trees and in the grass; that inner peace radiates in the creatures of the earth and in all living things and in the very air...That inner peace pervades all beings, all life and all existence.

There are discrete clouds here in the sky where the gentle sun sinks; and beside the tree on this hill the inflorescence sways in the breeze.

It is this silence and quiet that is peace past one's achievements and one's visions and affiliations and loyalties and past the words we utter and past the identity and comforts and security we crave; it is this inward gentleness in which the thoughts of the self cease…this is the precious pearl to which nothing else is equal…